Dr. Funster's
WORD BENDERS™ C1

Thinking and Vocabulary Fun

Titles in this series
Word Benders A1
Word Benders B1
Word Benders C1

Howard Black & Sandra Parks

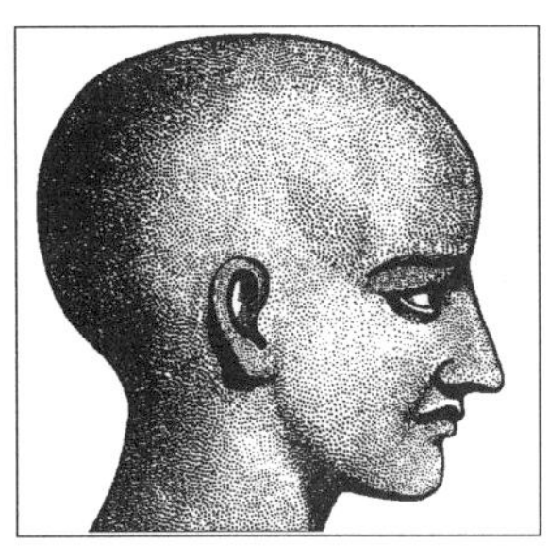

© 2003, 1983
CRITICAL THINKING BOOKS & SOFTWARE
www.CriticalThinking.com
P.O. Box 448 • Pacific Grove • CA 93950-0448
Phone 800-458-4849
ISBN 0-89455-814-5
Printed in the United States of America

About Dr. Funster's WORD BENDERS™

The *Word Benders* series promotes vocabulary acquisition, spelling skills, and deductive reasoning ability. *Word Benders* are letter systems in which some letters must change and others must remain the same. As students follow these rules, new words emerge. Students may use clues from the Definitions Box to decide the correct letter change or to verify the meaning of an unknown word formed by following the letter pattern. This game-like format encourages students to recognize and change word roots, prefixes, and suffixes to create new words.

The activities in this series are perfect for school, home, and travel. They are very popular as brain-start, extra credit, sponge, or reward activities, and will improve academic performance and raise test-taking ability for students at all grade levels.

Dr. Funster's Series Titles

Think-A-Minutes A1, A2, B1, B2, C1, C2

Word Benders A1, B1, C1

Visual Mind Benders A1, B1, C1

Creative Thinking Puzzlers A1, B1, C1

Quick Thinks Math A1, B1, C1

SIMILARITIES

Word Benders are word series in which each word is similar to the one preceding it. The blank circles indicate the letters to be changed; the letters that stay the same are shown by blank lines. The Definitions Box gives the meanings of the words in the word series, not in order. The Definitions Box can be used for clues and should be used to check your answers. Here is an example:

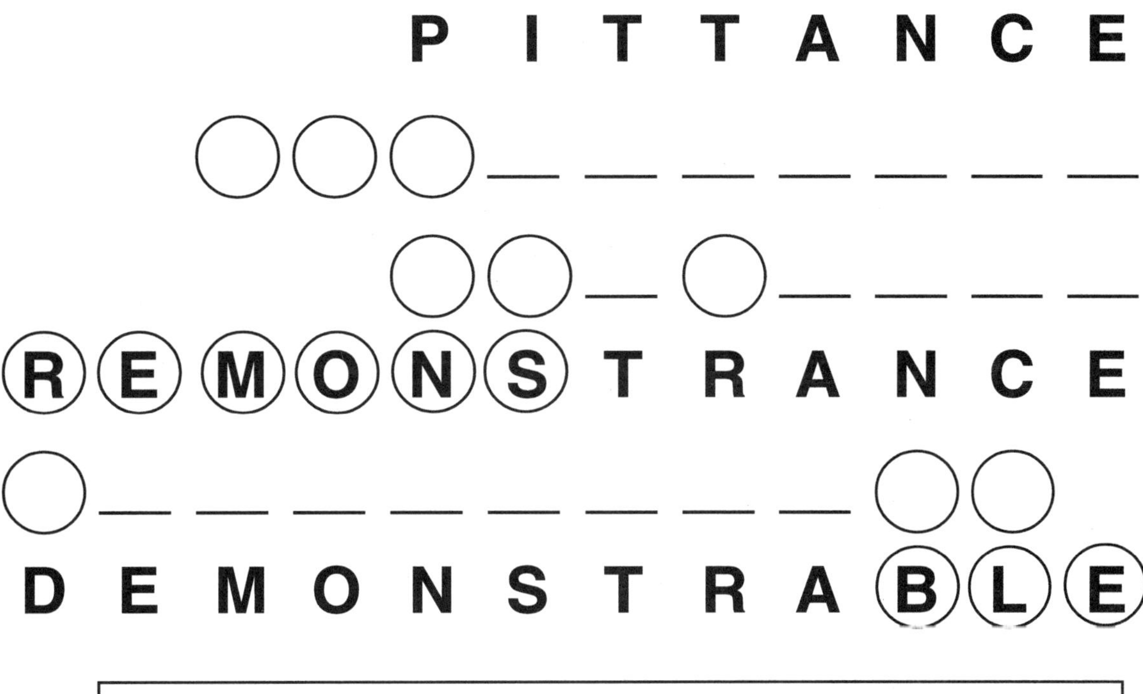

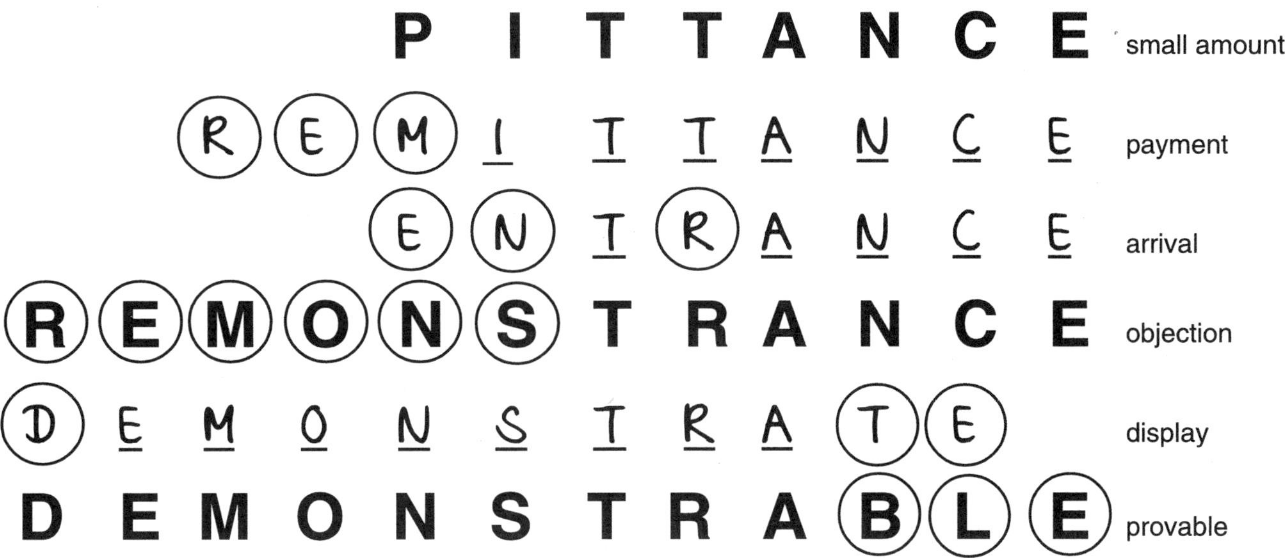

The answers with their definitions are:

P I T T A N C E	small amount
R E M I T T A N C E	payment
E N T R A N C E	arrival
R E M O N S T R A N C E	objection
D E M O N S T R A T E	display
D E M O N S T R A B L E	provable

DEFINITIONS BOX
arrival; display; objection; payment; provable; small amount

WORDS AND PHRASES

DIRECTIONS: Add or remove letters to complete the following phrases. Change only the letters that go in the circles.

1.

C L U T C H   HIT

RABBIT ◯ __ __ __ __

◯ __ __ __ __   MASTER PAINTER

CANE OR __ ◯ __ __ __ __

__ __ __ ◯ __ __ ◯   PEANUT BUTTER

◯ __ __ __ __   OF GRAPES

◯ __ __ __ __   TIME

LEFT IN A __ __ ◯ __ __

__ ◯ __ __ __ __   PEW

SEA __ __ __ __ ◯ ◯

◯ __ __ __   RIVAL

◯ __ __ __ __   IN STEP

◯ ◯ __ __ __   BARK CANOE

TAR ◯ __ ◯ __ __

__ __ __ __ __ ◯ ◯   AND CATCHER

(Continued)

__ __ __ __ __ ◯ ◯ AND CATCHER

SEVEN YEAR __ __ __ __

◯ ◯ __ __ __ __ IN TIME

__ __ ◯ __ ◯ OF THE UNION

BUS __ __ __ __ ◯ ◯ ◯

GAS ◯ __ __ __ __ __

◯ __ __ __ __ __ WIDE

STRANGE __ ◯ __ __ __ __

◯ __ __ __ __ DETECTOR

◯ ◯ ◯ __ __ __ __ __ TO DUTY

__ __ __ __ __ ◯ YOUR EFFORT

__ __ ◯ __ __ __ ◯ TO PRIVATE

◯ __ __ __ __ __ CONTROL

__ __ __ __ ◯ __ YOUR PAYMENT

DON'T BE __ __ __ __ ◯ ◯

◯ ◯ ◯ __ __ __ __ THE CLASS

D I S M A L SHOWING

SIMILARITIES

DIRECTIONS: Change or add only the letters that go in the circles. The words and phrases in the Definitions Box give meanings for the words being formed (not in order).

2.

R E L A T E

A V E N U E

DEFINITIONS BOX

boulevard; enjoy; income; having similar
characteristics; insight; kin; statistical relationship; tell

SIMILARITIES

DIRECTIONS: Change or add only the letters that go in the circles. The words and phrases in the Definitions Box give meanings for the words being formed (not in order).

3.

I M I T A T E

A N I M A L

M A X I M I Z A T I O N

DEFINITIONS BOX

beast; enlarge; enliven; highest degree; least;
lessen; liveliness; mimic; simulation

SIMILARITIES

DIRECTIONS: Change or add only the letters that go in the circles. The words and phrases in the Definitions Box give meanings for the words being formed (not in order).

4. P E R S I S T E N C E

◯◯◯ — — — — — — — — — —

◯◯ — — — — ◯ — — —

◯ — — — — — — — —

— — — — — —

◯◯ — — — — —

◯◯ — — — —

Ⓔ Ⓝ T R A N C E

DEFINITIONS BOX
admittance; dreamlike state; firmness; opposition;
perseverance; posture; quick look; separation

SIMILARITIES

DIRECTIONS: Change or add only the letters that go in the circles. The words and phrases in the Definitions Box give meanings for the words being formed (not in order).

5.

A L L U D E

_ _ _ _ ◯ _

_ _ _ ◯◯ ◯

◯ _ _ _ _ _

_ _ _ _ ◯◯ ◯◯

Ⓟ A L L E T

_ _ _ _ ◯◯ ◯

◯ ◯ ◯ _ _ _

S Q U A L Ⓞ Ⓡ

DEFINITIONS BOX

attraction; lack of color; permit; platform;
poverty; purse; rainstorm; refer to; roll

SIMILARITIES

DIRECTIONS: Change or add only the letters that go in the circles. The words and phrases in the Definitions Box give meanings for the words being formed (not in order).

6.

V E R S E

⃝⃝ — — — —

— — — — — — ⃝⃝⃝⃝

⃝⃝⃝ — — — — — — —

— — — — — — — ⃝⃝

⃝⃝ — — — — —

⃝⃝⃝ — — — — ⃝

— — — — ⃝

⃝⃝ — — — —

— — — — — ⃝⃝ — —

Ⓒ Ⓞ N V E R S I O N

DEFINITIONS BOX

able to be changed; detrimental; dunking; loathing; opposite; poetry;
refer to; remodeling; reversal of position; turn upside down; washable

---

SIMILARITIES

DIRECTIONS: Change or add only the letters that go in the circles. The words and phrases in the Definitions Box give meanings for the words being formed (not in order).

7. I N T E R V I E W

I N V E S T M E N T

DEFINITIONS BOX

anger; commitment of money; controversy; forestalling; innovation;
intercede; interference; meeting of delegates; question; satisfaction;

SIMILARITIES

DIRECTIONS: Change or add only the letters that go in the circles. The words and phrases in the Definitions Box give meanings for the words being formed (not in order).

8.

F R A C T I O N

C O N S T R U C T I O N

R E S T R I C T

DEFINITIONS BOX

architecture; build; confining; conflict of opinion; control;
damaging; force; limit; limitation; part; repression; ruin

SIMILARITIES

DIRECTIONS: Change or add only the letters that go in the circles. The words and phrases in the Definitions Box give meanings for the words being formed (not in order).

9.

A V E N U E

D I V E R G E

I N A D V E R T E N T

DEFINITIONS BOX

alteration; boulevard; distract; income; knowledgeable; meet;
opponent; retaliation; separate; speak; turn back; unintentional; vindicate

---

SIMILARITIES

DIRECTIONS: Change or add only the letters that go in the circles. The words and phrases in the Definitions Box give meanings for the words being formed (not in order).

10.

P R O R A T E

D E L U X E

S L U M P

DEFINITIONS BOX

apportion; chubby; collapse suddenly; constant change; elegant; flood; high-ranking clergy; introductory event; mislead; narrow gap; ornamental feather; stroke of luck

---

SIMILARITIES

DIRECTIONS: Change or add only the letters that go in the circles. The words and phrases in the Definitions Box give meanings for the words being formed (not in order).

11.

C O N C E R T

R E C O R D

C A V E A T

DEFINITIONS BOX

chorus; conflict; distinguish; document; find;
frolic; get rid of; interest; secret; shelter; warning

SIMILARITIES

DIRECTIONS: Change or add only the letters that go in the circles. The words and phrases in the Definitions Box give meanings for the words being formed (not in order).

12. C O M M O N

_ _ _ _ _ ◯ _ ◯

_ _ _ _ _ _ ◯

_ _ _ _ _ ◯ _ ◯

_ _ _ _ _ _ ◯ _

_ _ _ _ ◯ ◯ _

_ _ _ _ _ _ _ ◯ ◯ ◯ ◯

_ _ _ _ _ _ _ _ ◯ ◯

_ _ _ _ _ ◯ ◯ _ _ _

_ _ _ _ _ _ _ _ ◯ ◯ ◯ ◯

C   O M M U N I C A Ⓑ Ⓛ Ⓔ

<table>
<tr><td colspan="2" align="center">DEFINITIONS BOX</td></tr>
<tr><td colspan="2">covered washstand; group of people; impart information; infectious; merchandise; ordinary; praise; remark; replace with something else; society; spacious</td></tr>
</table>

SIMILARITIES

DIRECTIONS: Change or add only the letters that go in the circles. The words and phrases in the Definitions Box give meanings for the words being formed (not in order).

13. I N T E R F E R E N C E

R E F E R

P R O F E S S I O N

DEFINITIONS BOX

acknowledgement; admit; allowance; award; craft; credentials;
deduction; honor; intervention; parade; seminar; submit; yield

SIMILARITIES

DIRECTIONS: Change or add only the letters that go in the circles. The words and phrases in the Definitions Box give meanings for the words being formed (not in order).

14.

C A N I N E

M O R T G A G E

R O U T I N E

DEFINITIONS BOX

delighted; doglike; five voices; gate; hire; human; infuriate; malaria medicine;
omen; on the way; plaster; procedure; property agreement; purpose; satisfied

SIMILARITIES

DIRECTIONS: Change or add only the letters that go in the circles. The words and phrases in the Definitions Box give meanings for the words being formed (not in order).

15.

S T A G N A T E

_ _ _ _ _ _ ◯◯

◯◯ _ _ ◯ _ _ _

_ ◯ _ _ _ _ _

©Ⓞ Ⓝ F L A G R A Ⓣ Ⓘ Ⓞ Ⓝ

◯◯◯◯ _ _ _ _ _ _ _

◯◯◯ _ _ _ _ _ _ _ _ _ _ _ _

_ _ _ _ _ _ _ ◯◯◯ _

_ _ _ _ _ _ _ _ _

_ _ _ _ _◯◯◯◯◯◯◯

◯◯◯ _ _ _ _ _ _ _

◯ _ _ _ _ _ _ _

◯◯ _ _ _ _ _ _

Ⓒ I Ⓡ C Ⓤ Ⓜ F E R E N C E

DEFINITIONS BOX
apathy; aromatic; benefit; bold; circle perimeter; decomposition;
fail to develop; hindrance; honor; inactive; inferno; judgement; meeting; unification

---

SIMILARITIES

DIRECTIONS: Change or add only the letters that go in the circles. The words and phrases in the Definitions Box give meanings for the words being formed (not in order).

16.

E L E V A T E

E S C A L A T I O N

DEFINITIONS BOX

air circulation; comfort; disfigurement; expansion; happiness;
height; intensification; lift; material for reducing leakage; prophecy

SIMILARITIES

DIRECTIONS: Change or add only the letters that go in the circles. The words and phrases in the Definitions Box give meanings for the words being formed (not in order).

17.

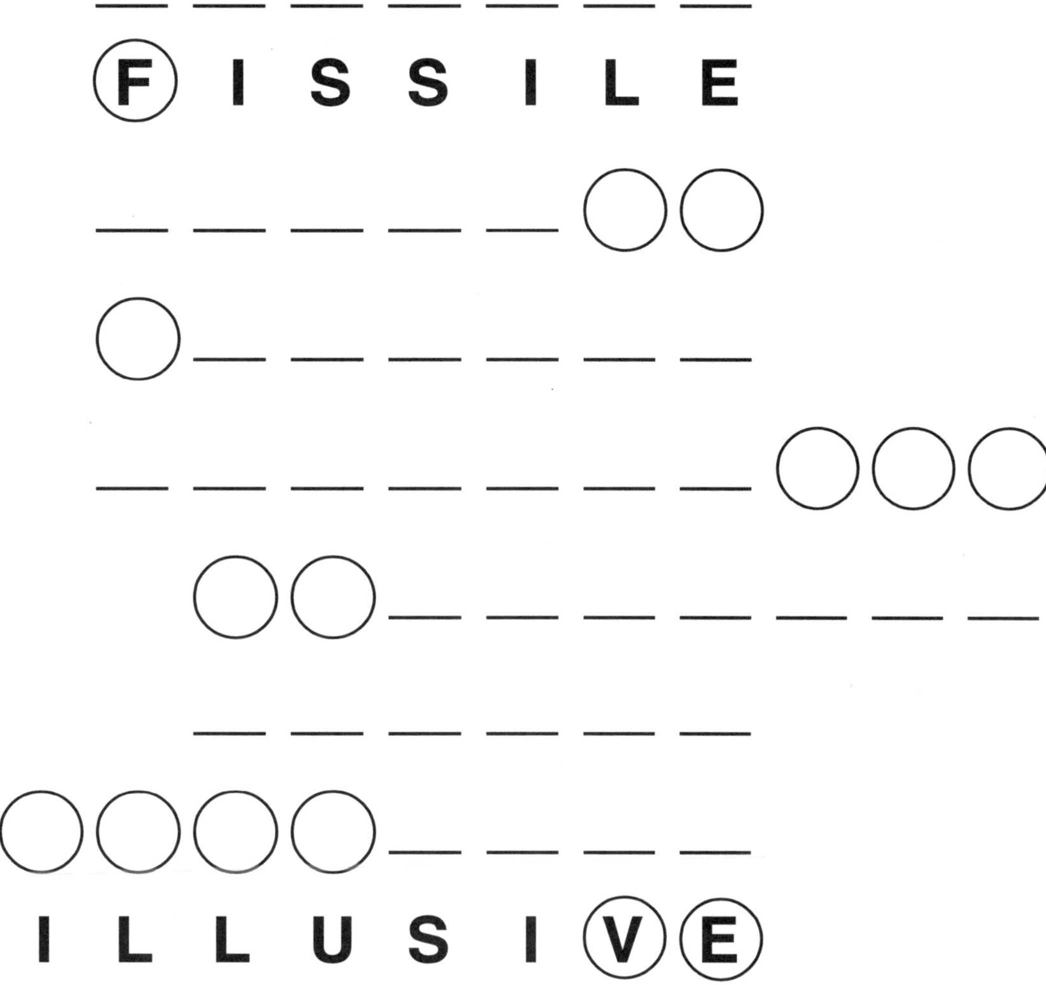

DEFINITIONS BOX

capable of fission; deceptive; evangelist; idealist;
mirage; projectile; revelation; splitting apart; task

SIMILARITIES

DIRECTIONS: Change or add only the letters that go in the circles. The words and phrases in the Definitions Box give meanings for the words being formed (not in order).

18.

D E P R E S S I O N

S U C C E S S I (V) (E)

R E C E (P) (T) I (V) (E)

U N C E R T A I N (T) (Y)

DEFINITIONS BOX

accepting; admission; consecutive; contraction; control by force; discover; doubt; eloquent; extravagant; order; receiving; restrictive; reversion; revision; rising; sadness; slump; unstable

SIMILARITIES

DIRECTIONS: Change or add only the letters that go in the circles. The words and phrases in the Definitions Box give meanings for the words being formed (not in order).

19.

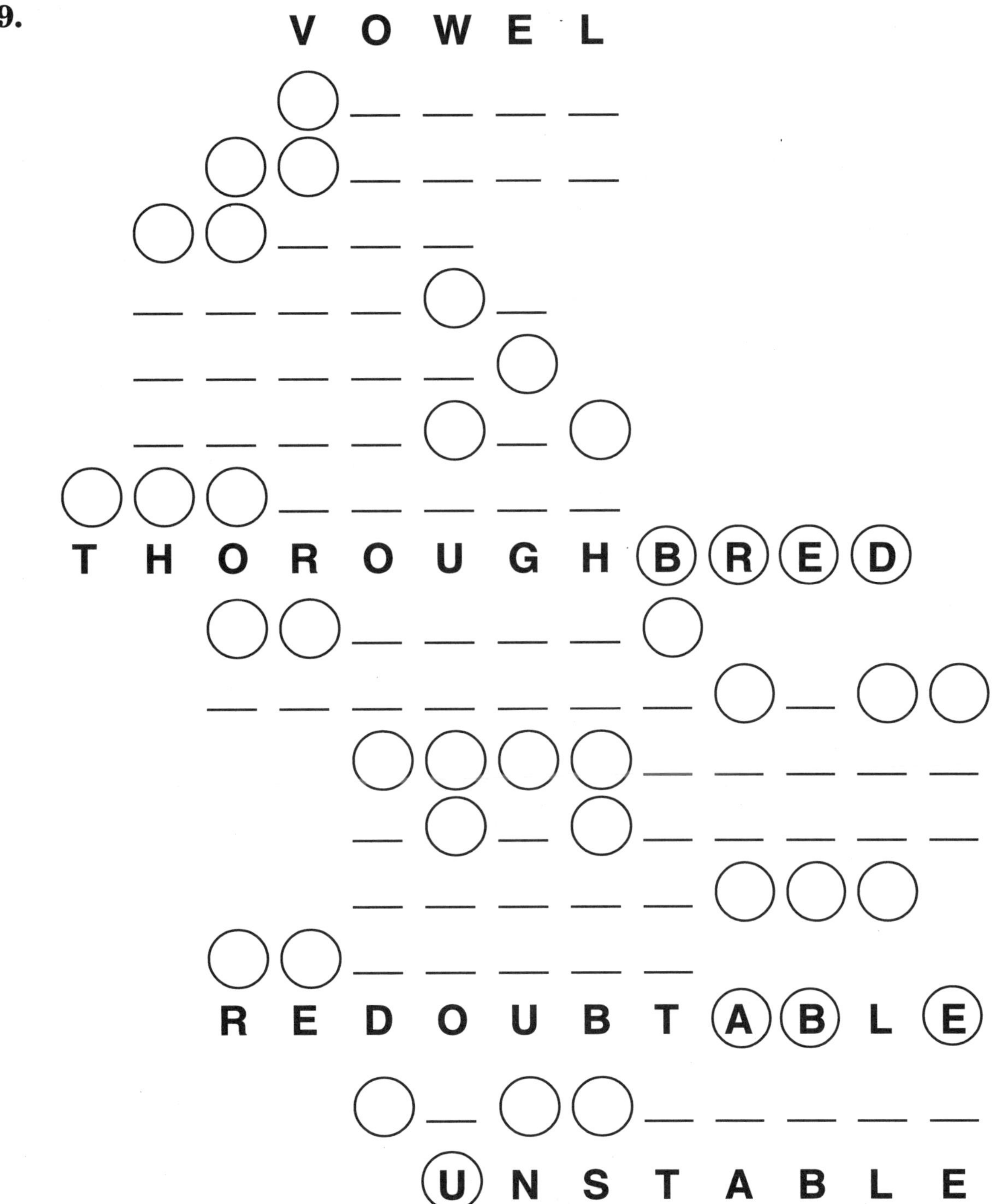

DEFINITIONS BOX

drying cloth; enclosed fortification; fearless; formidable; idea;
king's chair; letter; multitude; painstaking; peace officer; penetrating;
pure stock; spade; toss; uncertain; unquestionably; unthinking; volatile

---

SIMILARITIES

DIRECTIONS: Change or add only the letters that go in the circles. The words and phrases in the Definitions Box give meanings for the words being formed (not in order).

20.

R E Q U I S I T I O N

C O N D I T I O N

I N T U I T I O N

DEFINITIONS BOX

attitude; combining word; completion; demand; fee for instruction; inquiry;
insight; journey; personality; printing; restore; stipulation; suggestion; written testimony

SIMILARITIES

DIRECTIONS: Change or add only the letters that go in the circles. The words and phrases in the Definitions Box give meanings for the words being formed (not in order).

21.

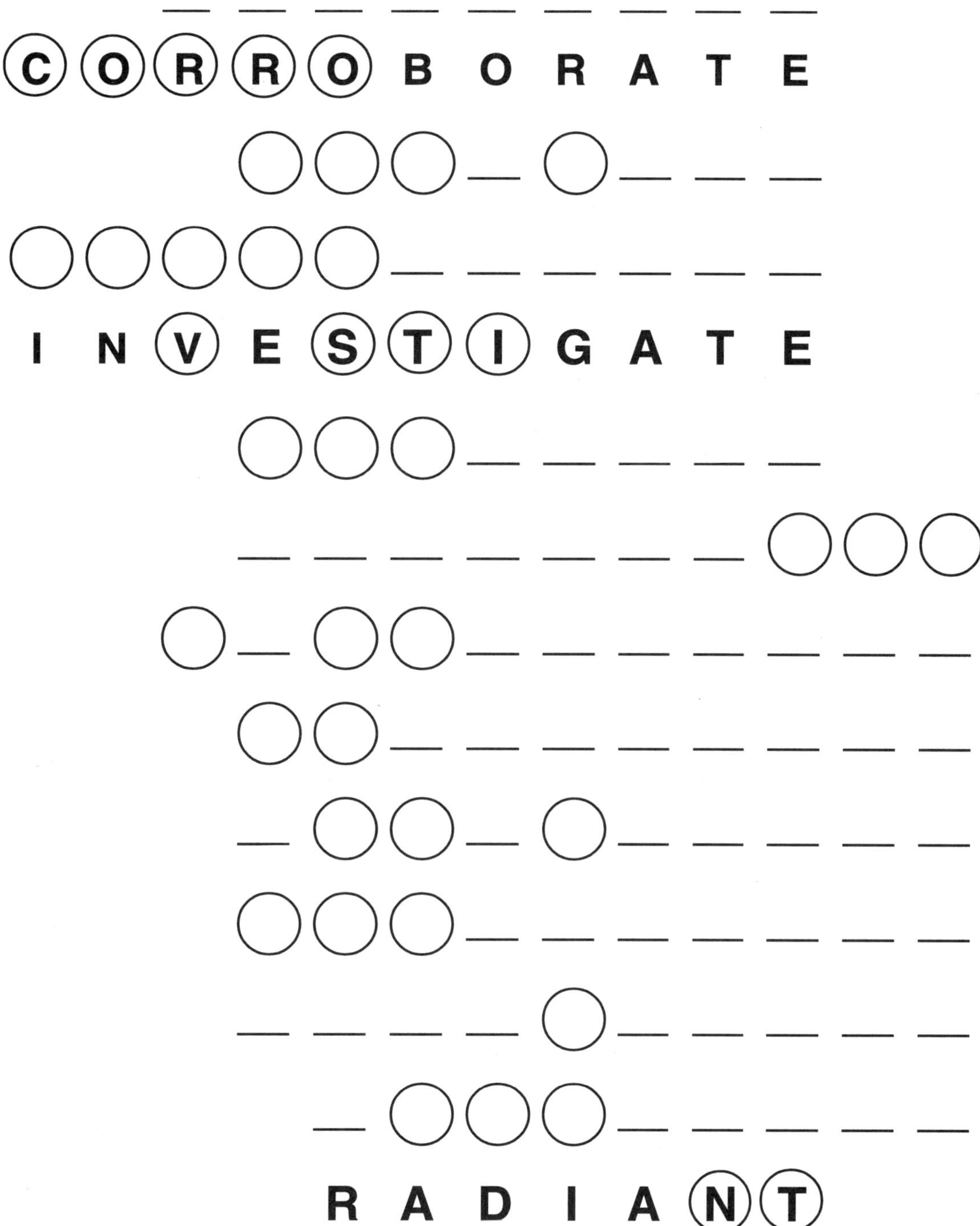

DEFINITIONS BOX

aggravation; annul; beaming; confirm; emission; explore; fancy;
guide a ship; lawsuit; question; rising; stimulus; voyage plan; water

SIMILARITIES

DIRECTIONS: Change or add only the letters that go in the circles. The words and phrases in the Definitions Box give meanings for the words being formed (not in order).

22.

R A M P A G E

I N D E P E N D E N T

C O N V E N I E N T

DEFINITIONS BOX

accessible; assertion; contrive; deviate; dubious claim; fortified wall;
free; hindrance; plan; set in; spree; subordinate; thwart; treaty; trust; unrestrained

SIMILARITIES

DIRECTIONS: Change or add only the letters that go in the circles. The words and phrases in the Definitions Box give meanings for the words being formed (not in order).

23.

S U R V I V E

I N F R A C T I O N

DEFINITIONS BOX

bending; blemished; candy; deliberation; desertion; endure; failure to comply; flaw; inmate; lively; principle; productive; reawakening; resuscitate; rising air; thoughtful

SIMILARITIES

DIRECTIONS: Change or add only the letters that go in the circles. The words and phrases in the Definitions Box give meanings for the words being formed (not in order).

24.

S U P E R

P R E T E N S E

(Continued)

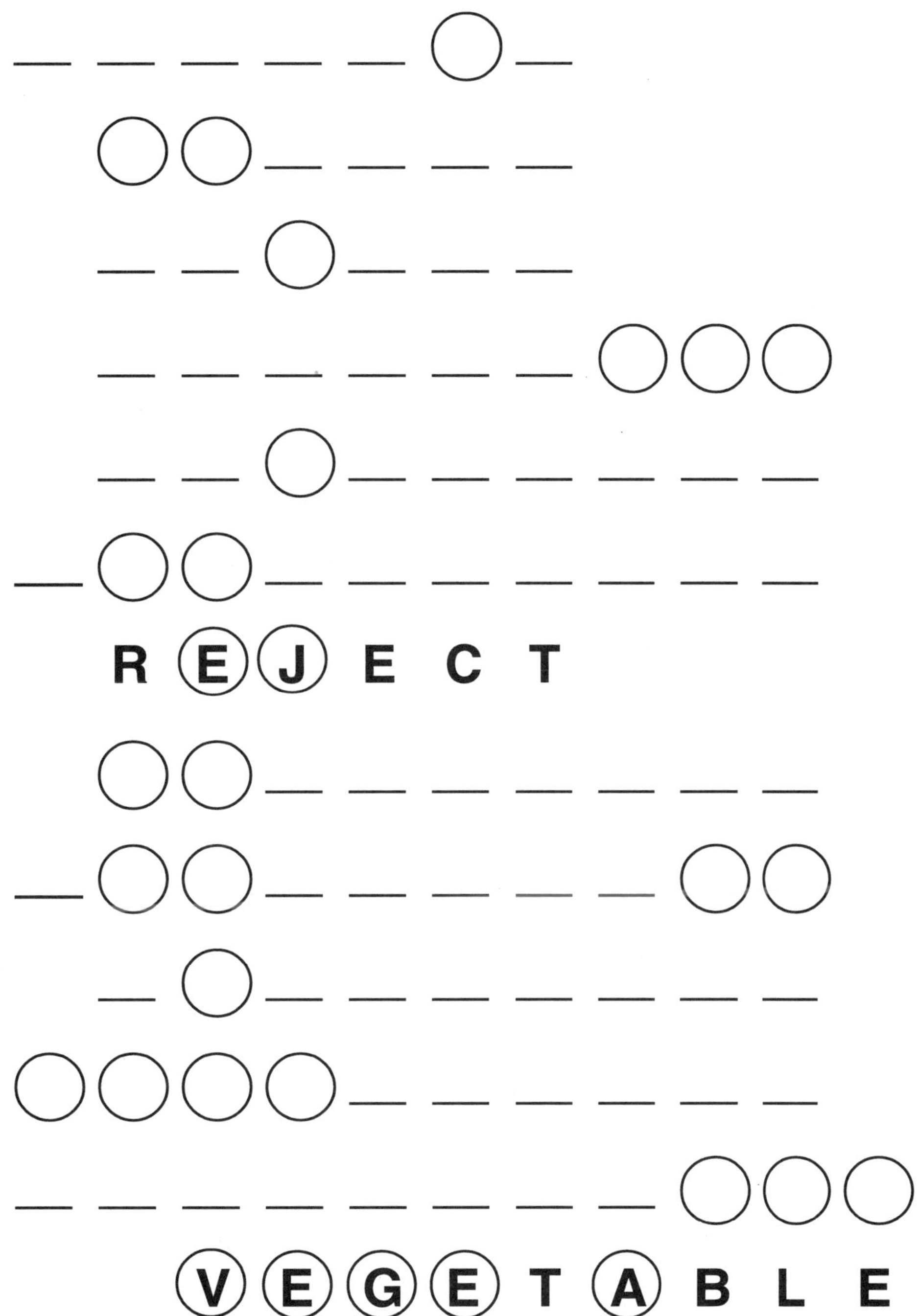

DEFINITIONS BOX

better; brotherly; concentrated; defend; denial; disguise; dismiss; edible plant; everlasting; extension; fault; find; forever; gathering; great; imperfect; inside; investigator; lesser; men's society; modifier; object; outside; peripheral; shielding; trainee; worth keeping

Here is a grid to use for constructing your own Word Bender.

ANSWERS

1. **CLUTCH** HIT
   RABBIT **H**UTCH
   DUTCH MASTER PAINTER
   CANE OR **CR**UTCH
   CRUN**CH**Y PEANUT BUTTER
   BUNCH OF GRAPES
   L**UNCH** TIME
   LEFT IN A L**URCH**
   CH**URCH** PEW
   SEA URCH**IN**
   A**RCH** RIVAL
   MARCH IN STEP
   BIRCH BARK CANOE
   TAR **PIT**CH
   PITCH**ER** AND CATCHER
   SEVEN YEAR **ITCH**
   STITCH IN TIME
   ST**ATE** OF THE UNION
   BUS ST**ATION**
   GAS RATION
   NATION WIDE
   STRANGE N**OTION**
   M**OTION** DETECTOR
   DEVOTION TO DUTY
   DEVOT**E** YOUR EFFORT
   DEMOTE**D** TO PRIVATE
   REMOTE CONTROL
   REM**IT** YOUR PAYMENT
   DON'T BE REM**ISS**
   DISMISS THE CLASS
   DISMAL SHOWING

2. **RELATE** (tell)
   CORRELATE (having similar characteristics)
   CORRELAT**ION** (statistical relationship)
   RELATION (kin)
   REVELATION (insight)
   REVEL (enjoy)
   REVE**NUE** (income)
   AVENUE (boulevard)

3. **IMITATE** (mimic)
   IMITAT**ION** (simulation)
   ANIMATION (liveliness)
   ANIMATE (enliven)
   ANIMAL (beast)
   MINIMAL (least)
   MINIM**IZE** (lessen)
   MA**X**IMIZE (enlarge)
   MAXIMIZATION (highest degree)

4. **PERSISTENCE** (perseverance)
   CONSISTENCE (firmness)
   RESISTANCE (opposition)
   DISTANCE (separation)
   STANCE (posture)
   GLANCE (quick look)

5. **ALLUDE** (refer to)
   ALLURE (attraction)
   ALL**OW** (permit)
   WALLOW (roll)
   WALL**ET** (purse)
   PALLET (platform)
   PALL**OR** (lack of color)
   SQUALL (rainstorm)
   SQUALOR (poverty)

6. **VERSE** (poetry)
   REVERSE (opposite)
   REVERS**IBLE** (able to be changed)
   IMMERSIBLE (washable)
   IMMERSI**ON** (dunking)
   AVERSION (loathing)
   ADVERSE (detrimental)
   ADVER**T** (refer to)
   INVERT (turn upside down)
   INVER**S**ION (a reversal of position)
   CONVERSION (remodeling)

7. **INTERVIEW** (question)
   INTERV**ENE** (intercede)
   INTERVEN**TION** (interference)
   INVENTION (innovation)
   PREVENTION (forestalling)
   CONVENTION (meeting of delegates)
   CONTENTION (controversy)
   CONTENT**MENT** (satisfaction)
   RESENTMENT (anger)
   INVESTMENT (commitment of money)

8. **FRACTION** (part)
   FRICTION (conflict of opinion)
   RESTRICTION (limitation)
   RESTRICTI**VE** (confining)
   DESTRUCTIVE (damaging)
   DESTRUCTI**ON** (ruin)
   CONSTRUCTION (architecture)
   CONSTRUCT (build)
   CONSTR**AIN** (force)
   CONSTRAINT (repression)
   RESTRAINT (control)
   RESTRICT (limit)

9. **AVENUE** (boulevard)
   AVEN**GE** (vindicate)
   REVENGE (retaliation)
   REVENUE (income)
   REVER**T** (turn back)
   DIVERT (distract)
   TRANCE (dreamlike state)
   ENTRANCE (admittance)

10. **PRORATE** (apportion)
    PR**EL**ATE (high-ranking clergy)
    PREL**UDE** (introductory event)
    DELUDE (mislead)
    DELU**GE** (flood)
    DELUXE (elegant)
    FLUX (constant change)
    FLUKE (stroke of luck)
    FLUME (narrow gap)
    PLUME (ornamental feather)
    PLUM**P** (chubby)
    SLUMP (collapse suddenly)

11. **CONCERT** (chorus)
    CONCERN (interest)
    DISCERN (distinguish)
    DISC**ARD** (get rid of)
    DISCORD (conflict)
    RECORD (document)
    RECO**VER** (find)
    COVER (shelter)
    COVER**T** (secret)
    CA**V**ORT (frolic)
    CAVEAT (warning)

12. **COMMON** (ordinary)
    COMM**ENT** (remark)
    COMMEND (praise)
    COMM**UNE** (group of people)
    COMMUT**E** (substitute)
    COMMO**D**E (covered washstand)
    COMMOD**IOUS** (spacious)
    COMMODI**TY** (merchandise)
    COMMUNITY (society)
    COMMUNI**CATE** (impart information)
    COMMUNICABLE (infectious)

13. **INTERFERENCE** (intervention)
    DEFERENCE (honor)
    INFERENCE (deduction)
    CONFERENCE (seminar)
    REFERENCE (credentials)
    REFER (submit)
    DEFER (yield)
    CONFER (award)
    CONFE**SS** (admit)
    CONFESS**ION** (acknowledgement)
    CONCESSION (allowance)
    PROCESSION (parade)
    PROFESSION (craft)

14. **CANINE** (doglike)
    QUININE (malaria medicine)
    QUINTET (five voices)
    INTENT (purpose)
    CONTENT (satisfied)
    PORTENT (omen)
    PORTAL (gate)
    MORTAL (human)
    MORTAR (plaster)
    MORTGAGE (property
       agreement)
    ENGAGE (hire)
    ENRAGE (infuriate)
    ENRAPT (delighted)
    ENROUTE (on the way)
    ROUTINE (procedure)

15. **STAGNATE** (fail to develop)
    STAGNANT (inactive)
    FRAGRANT (aromatic)
    FLAGRANT (bold)
    CONFLAGRATION (inferno)
    INTEGRATION (unification)
    DISINTEGRATION
       (decomposition)
    DISINTEREST (apathy)
    INTEREST (benefit)
    INTERFERENCE (hindrance)
    CONFERENCE (meeting)
    INFERENCE (judgement)
    DEFERENCE (honor)
    CIRCUMFERENCE (circle
       perimeter)

16. **ELEVATE** (lift)
    ELEVATION (height)
    INSULATION (material for
       reducing leakage)
    CONSOLATION (comfort)
    MUTILATION (disfigurement)
    VENTILATION (air circulation)
    DILATION (expansion)
    ELATION (happiness)
    REVELATION (prophecy)
    ESCALATION (intensification)

17. MISSILE (projectile)
    FISSILE (capable of fission)
    FISSION (splitting apart)
    MISSION (task)
    MISSIONARY (evangelist)
    VISIONARY (idealist)
    VISION (revelation)
    ILLUSION (mirage)
    ILLUSIVE (deceptive)

18. **DEPRESSION** (sadness)
    REGRESSION (reversion)
    CONFESSION (admission)
    SUCCESSION (order)
    SUCCESSIVE (consecutive)

EXCESSIVE (extravagant)
EXPRESSIVE (eloquent)
REPRESSIVE (restrictive)
REPRESSION (control by force)
COMPRESSION (contraction)
RECESSION (slump)
RECEPTIVE (accepting)
RECEPTION (receiving)
RECENSION (revision)
ASCENSION (rising)
ASCERTAIN (discover)
UNCERTAIN (unstable)
UNCERTAINTY (doubt)

19. **VOWEL** (letter)
    TOWEL (drying cloth)
    TROWEL (spade)
    THROW (toss)
    THRONE (king's chair)
    THRONG (multitude)
    THROUGH (penetrating)
    THOROUGH (painstaking)
    THOROUGHBRED (pure stock)
    THOUGHT (idea)
    THOUGHTLESS (unthinking)
    DAUNTLESS (fearless)
    DOUBTLESS
       (unquestionably)
    DOUBTFUL (uncertain)
    REDOUBT (enclosed
       fortification)
    REDOUBTABLE (formidable)
    CONSTABLE (peace officer)
    UNSTABLE (volatile)

20. **REQUISITION** (demand)
    INQUISITION (inquiry)
    POSITION (attitude)
    DEPOSITION (written
       testimony)
    DISPOSITION (personality)
    PROPOSITION (suggestion)
    PREPOSITION (combining
       word)
    CONDITION (stipulation)
    RECONDITION (restore)
    EXPEDITION (journey)
    EDITION (printing)
    FRUITION (completion)
    TUITION (fee for instruction)
    INTUITION (insight)

21. ELABORATE (fancy)
    CORROBORATE (confirm)
    ABROGATE (annul)
    INTERROGATE (question)
    INVESTIGATE (explore)
    NAVIGATE (guide a ship)
    NAVIGATION (voyage plan)
    INSTIGATION (stimulus)
    LITIGATION (lawsuit)
    LEVITATION (rising)
    IRRITATION (aggravation)

IRRIGATION (water)
RADIATION (emission)
RADIANT (beaming)

22. **RAMPAGE** (spree)
    RAMPANT (unrestrained)
    RAMPART (fortified wall)
    DEPART (deviate)
    DEPEND (trust)
    DEPENDENT (subordinate)
    INDEPENDENT (free)
    INDENT (set in)
    INTENT (plan)
    INVENT (contrive)
    PREVENT (thwart)
    PREVENTION (hindrance)
    PRETENSION (dubious claim)
    CONTENTION (assertion)
    CONVENTION (treaty)
    CONVENIENT (accessible)

23. **SURVIVE** (endure)
    REVIVE (resuscitate)
    REVIVING (reawakening)
    CONVIVIAL (lively)
    CONVICT (inmate)
    CONVICTION (principle)
    CONVECTION (rising air)
    CONFECTION (candy)
    DEFECTION (desertion)
    DEFECT (flaw)
    DEFECTIVE (blemished)
    EFFECTIVE (productive)
    REFLECTIVE (thoughtful)
    REFLECTION (deliberation)
    REFRACTION (bending)
    INFRACTION (failure to comply)

24. **SUPER** (great)
    SUPERIOR (better)
    INFERIOR (lesser)
    INTERIOR (inside)
    EXTERIOR (outside)
    EXTERNAL (peripheral)
    ETERNAL (everlasting)
    FRATERNAL (brotherly)
    FRATERNITY (men's society)
    ETERNITY (forever)
    INTERN (trainee)
    INTENSE (concentrated)
    PRETENSE (disguise)
    PROTEST (object)
    PROTECT (defend)
    DETECT (find)
    DEFECT (fault)
    DEFECTIVE (imperfect)
    DETECTIVE (investigator)
    PROTECTIVE (shielding)
    REJECT (dismiss)
    ADJECTIVE (modifier)
    PROJECTION (extension)
    REJECTION (denial)
    COLLECTION (gathering)
    COLLECTIBLE (worth keeping)
    VEGETABLE (edible plant)

